Healing Waters

A Life of Hardships, Faith, and
Family

Brady Busby

ISBN: 9781983036798

DEDICATION

For my sweet Ashley

Table of Contents

Healing Waters

ACKNOWLEDGMENTS

Thank you to all my friends and family who encouraged
me to write this book and keep at it. I'm grateful for all
the editing to the memoir
and for the assistance in getting my thoughts into a
readable form.

CHAPTER 1

Mission First

The attack started from the back gate of our base, directly across from an airstrip where my fellow soldiers and I were going about our daily duties. We were inside a building when items suddenly flew off the walls. The first blast came from a VBIED (vehicle-born improvised explosive device), followed by several teams of suicide bombers with RPGs (rocket-propelled grenades) trying to breach the base.

It was June 2010 and my third tour in Afghanistan. I had done multiple tours in Iraq and served on peacekeeping missions in Kosovo for the U.S. military. But I had never faced an onslaught like this, which I would soon realize would set the pace for the rest of my deployment.

I was just about to finish handing off duties to another team when the complex attack began. After getting my soldiers in a bunker, I rushed to get a better vantage point for the attack, seeing only smoke but hearing a firefight below.

A pair of Apache and Kiowa helicopters arrived, making me feel a little safer. But the attack was still unfolding, with one round whizzing past me.

A second car approached the base, with soldiers rushing to kill the driver before he could get close enough to possibly detonate the vehicle. The car came to a halt, with several men exiting the vehicle and again trying to breach the wall to get on base. Soon the helicopters began

unloading their guns on the attackers, bringing the fight to a speedy end.

During the next two months, our base was hit by a barrage of attacks. One night, we were conducting a mission when mortars started exploding nearby. I was standing outside one of our buildings, talking to another Army officer, when I suddenly heard a strange hissing noise followed by a very large explosion.

I felt heat and saw a bright light as shrapnel began to slam into everything around me. My ears rang, but I did not black out. After what seemed like several minutes, I made quick work of shepherding the soldiers under my command into a bunker, knowing another mortar was likely on its way. They never come solo, and unlike Iraq, where some of the older munitions that were being used were duds, these enemy mortars always seemed to fulfill their intended use.

"Get in the bunker!" I screamed to my team. "That was close." We got inside just before a second mortar hit. Lucky for us it hit the motor pool of the "other government agency" that was next to us. We stayed in the bunker until the last two landed farther away and then we went back to work. *"Mission First."*

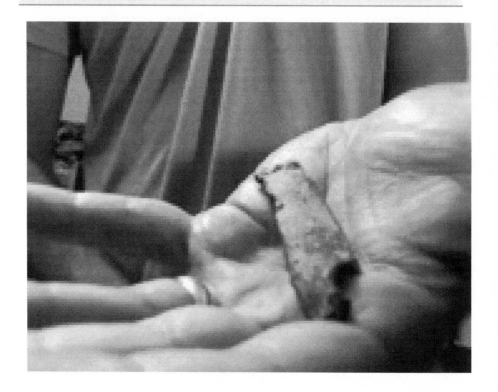

The next day I checked in at the aid station at the end of the base, but because I wasn't bleeding I seemed to be fine in the eyes of the medical units. I was essentially told to "Suck it up."

We continued to perform our missions for a few more months before I returned to Germany, where I had previously been stationed because my branch manager wanted to give me a break from deployments to the Middle East.

I wasn't home a week before my wife, Sarah, and I both realized something was wrong. I was not myself. I had nightmares where I would wake up in a cold sweat or would forget things and wake up not knowing where I was. I was always on alert—and angry. I was in a lot of physical pain as well. I could barely walk.

Sitting in an office on base waiting to talk to the Army psychiatrist, I filled out forms that asked me all sorts of questions about things that I was dealing with, physically and emotionally. While I filled them out, I knew that my career in military intelligence was over.

I was diagnosed with severe combat-related PTSD. I also had sustained a TBI, traumatic brain injury, from the mortar blast. Of all the concussions that I have had in my life, the last big one seemed to have caught up to me. I couldn't concentrate for days, with constant migraines, night sweats, nightmares and flashbacks. I was depressed, had guilt, embarrassment, and was on high alert at all times.

My unit didn't know what to do with me at that point. I couldn't work anymore because it would bring on anxiety attacks, so the unit gave me a job as the company XO or executive officer. It wasn't long before I was moved to a warrior transition unit once it was clear that I was not deployable anymore. My wife and two daughters were also having to deal with all the deployments, and it was taking a toll on them as well.

I was a mess and on so many drugs that my doctor told me that if I didn't get off of them I would be dead in five years. I was taking thirty-seven pills a day at one point. The fact that I was in constant pain didn't help. I was then sent to a mental hospital in Virginia for a month for an intensive inpatient PTSD program. This actually turned out to be a bad thing for me. I gained about twenty pounds in a month, my prescription drugs were all changed around, and I was walking around with a cane due to a severe limp that had begun even before gaining the weight. The extra pounds just added to my discomfort.

I did actually make some friends in the program that shared some similar experiences. But everything that the doctors tried to do for me didn't really do anything. I was actually worse when I got back to Germany.

Sarah, Ashley, and Emma—my girls—stayed by my side and actually found some comedy around my situation. I can remember getting ready for church the first time after getting back from the mental hospital. My pants didn't even come close to fitting. They were way too small, and Sarah got a good laugh about that one. I had never struggled with my weight before, being tall and thin all of my life.

And my difficulties only continued. I was getting a discography procedure at the pain clinic when the doctor completely ruptured my disk. Shortly after that, I was scheduled for a disk fusion in my L5-S1 area of my lower back. It required multiple surgeries.

My large team of doctors and my wife had planned behind my back to get me off the high dose of opiates and other drugs I was taking. I was not expecting an eight-day stay in the ICU, but that is what happened.

I had been on and off opioids for years at this point, but I was using so much that my body needed it to function. I was in bad shape, so it was the best thing for me. At the time I can remember being very angry, but at the same time I have very vivid memories and I am sure I acted rather crazy.

The first day in surgery went pretty well, but one of the titanium screws they drilled in was too close to my nerve. I remember coming to and being in the worst pain. They had tilted the table with my head down for the surgery which caused a major migraine on top of the pain from the surgery. I was on a high dose of Ketamine (horse tranquilizer) to bind to the opiates and wash them out of my system.

The next day they went back in and replaced the screw with a larger one that they drilled into a different location. After that surgery I was recovering when I had a bad nightmare. All my monitors went off and I was in a lot of pain. They had me at the max dose of Ketamine and couldn't give me anything else. Sarah authorized the doctors to perform an experimental procedure to help my PTSD buy running a needle up my jugular and basically do a nerve block in my memory center.

I was in the ICU for eight rough days, but when they moved me to a normal room I was able to function on just seven Percocet a day. I tried acupuncture, TENS units, all kinds of treatments for my back and neck pain, but I was never able to fully come off of them. The medications just kept coming.

One nice thing that happened while I was recovering was when Gloria Gaynor visited me and told me that "You too will survive." We later watched her sing with me in a wheelchair holding our daughters, Ashley and Emma. They were getting older and didn't fit as well with all three of us, but I didn't care.

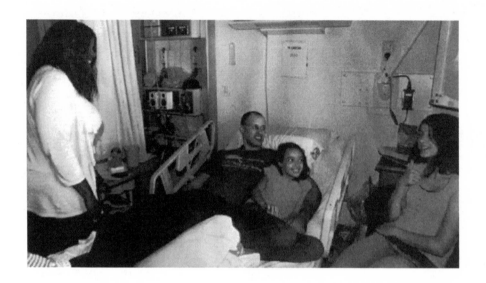

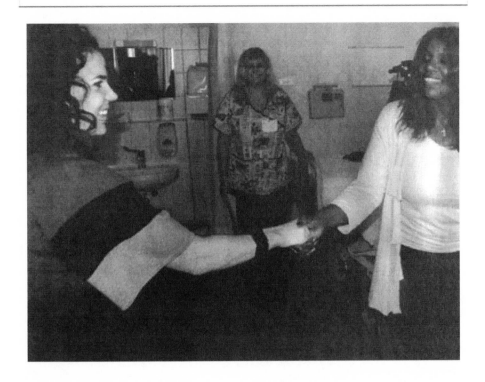

After over a year in the WTU, the doctors didn't really offer many options other than a medical retirement. I was retired at the age of thirty-eight. This was not how I expected my career in the Army to end.

Chapter 2

Humble Beginnings

I was born in Tyler, Texas, in 1974 to my parents, Max and Lynne Busby. Dad was building houses at the time, and Mom was a stay-at-home mom. I was the second oldest of what would eventually be six children. My brothers and I were all baptized in the Catholic church at Mother Frances Hospital in Tyler when we were born, even though my parents were long-standing members of The Church of Jesus Christ of the Latter Day Saints (LDS). I guess we have our bases covered. Bryan and I were actually named after towns in Texas. The town of Brady is in the center of Texas and is called the heart of Texas.

I do not remember that much about Tyler other than some distant memories about my dog, Peety, chasing me and my brother Bryan around. Petty got in a fight with the Doberman Pinscher from next door and lost. I can remember losing him, leaving me exposed to dealing with death at a young age.

My mom kept a journal around that time and some of the journal entries read:

"February 9, 1979. Brady is still quiet and plays by himself a good part of the day. He didn't want to go outside yesterday because he was afraid a bee would sting him!

Dad fixed your stick horse named Bucken Brody, and you would ride all over the house while Dad would try to rope you."

My first word was Riboflavin! My dad kept telling me to say it over and over again. My parents were happy to have a little black-haired boy with big blue eyes. However, my brother didn't like me very much.

My mom thought that something might be wrong with me because I was so quiet and observant. My brother Bryan on the other hand was a little devil child, although he will tell you otherwise.

Mom told me stories of how she had to nurse me in another room while he would throw a tantrum and kick the door until she was done. She also told me how he tried to jam tinfoil down my throat once before she could get to me. Word was, he didn't like me very much and tried to get rid of me several times when we were young.

My mother would tell us that my brother Bryan and I would sit and listen to the lightning and thunder in North East Texas and say, "We hear you, Godzilla."

I had my first traumatic experience of my life about that time. My family was moving to Arizona and I was driving with my dad and older brother, Bryan. The old station wagon we were driving in caught on fire. In the rush to get my brother and I out of the car, my dad threw me into the road with a semi-truck bearing down on me. The truck was able to stop in time and the driver got me to safety, but that is something that I still remember vividly.

We moved to a small village south of Holbrook, Arizona, called Woodruff. It was founded by the early members of The Church of Jesus Christ of Latter-Day Saints. We stayed with my Aunt Shirley and Uncle Jerald Scorse and all my cousin's when we first arrived, until we eventually found our own house. I attended school in a one-room schoolhouse that is now a museum.

Woodruff was an interesting place while I was growing up. A lot of relatives lived there, and it is a small mostly farming community. When I think of my childhood, I remember it being green with trees, and there was an irrigation ditch that went right by our tiny house. My mother tells me how I was always playing in the water and mud. One time, my brother and I painted a giant smiley face on the side of the house with that red northern Arizona mud. I believe it is still there today.

The home was built a long time before by my great-grandfather Gardner. He was a stonemason and helped to build the old one-room school house and worked on the local church. The house had to be renovated before our family could move in, but I have memories of "helping" my dad with the house when I was little.

Our new home was a little farm with a garden and a field to grow crops. We had a chicken coop, and a barn across the street full of hay. I can remember my dad milking the cow and squirting the milk right into my mouth. The property also had easy access to the little Colorado River and a grove of trees. This is where I would play and learned to fish. Playing was sometimes hard on my body, as my mother recalled.

I broke my arm after my brother told me to jump out of the tree swing:

"April 11 1980. Easter was full of surprises. Some of them good but mostly bad. Brady was swinging on a rope that was hanging over a limb of the cottonwood tree. He jumped off and landed on a rock and broke his arm! The minute I saw it you could tell it was broken. It looked like the pipe under the sink! Max took him to the hospital and got it put back together. He was back home in time to watch the second session of conference but poor Brady didn't wake up until about 8 p.m. I was supposed to take him in Tuesday for a cast check and had to go back twice. Finally, I got home and the doctor called and told me his X-rays showed he needed to have his bones reset and wanted me in Flagstaff that night. I told them I couldn't go that night and I'd have to be there in the morning…we got there about 11 a.m. and checked in. Brady's surgery was all done by six, and he was sleeping soundly. His night went really well and we went home the next morning.

He's now home and driving me crazy trying to keep his arm elevated and making him hold still...Brady can go back to school Monday so I hope he can make it for the next 6 weeks and not break anything else. He'll have to have his cast on for his birthday though and he's not too excited about that! Note...I remember I was so big and pregnant that everyone just kept telling me to sit down and not worry.

They didn't want to deliver a baby and fix a broken arm. Maxer was born on the 25th." (Mom always calls my youngest brother, Maxer.)

The schoolhouse was the main hang out spot for all the kids in the town. I remember the teacher being mean and slapping our hands with a ruler if we got out of line. I was the quiet angel child so I never got into trouble.

Mom recalls from her journal:

> "October 30, 1980. Brady has advanced three
> readers since school started and he's doing great. He
> loves school this year and you can tell by the way
> he's working."

> "November 20 1980. Brady is doing fine in school.
> He is more content at school than I've ever seen
> him."

The biggest building in the village was the church my
parents and family and I were members of —The Church
of Jesus Christ of Latter-Day Saints.

My older brother, Bryan, was baptized into the church
in the murky waters of the Little Colorado River.   He
recalls of the event:

> "I remember I went in wearing white and came out
> brown and had to walk home because dad didn't
> want me getting his car all wet so I walked home
> in the gravel road. I didn't have any shoes on and

my feet were hurting." He does admit that, "It was definitely a cool place to get baptized though. Very original."

My grandparents, Ollie and Robert Busby, also lived in Woodruff surrounded by many aunts, uncles, cousins and friends. Our family had fun climbing the butte (a volcanic cinder plume that is now mostly gone), searching for arrowheads, riding motorcycles and just spending time with together. I remember the hole in the ground across the street from my grandparent's small trailer home. It was to be someone's basement for a house at some point, but we loved playing in it.

My father worked as a DJ at a local AM radio station in nearby Holbrook, and we moved there when I was in the third grade. I went to school at Holbrook Elementary School. We lived in a small house. There were more kids by this point in time—my older brother, Bryan, and younger brothers, Bob and Max, and my two younger sisters, Holly and Leah.

We went to church in Holbrook as well, and when I
was eight years old I was placed under the water and was
baptized into the church as well. I can remember thinking

about how clean and pure I felt after my baptism. I went to church with my family every Sunday. In the LDS Church we take the sacrament every Sunday. It is to remind those who partake of it to be more Christ-like and to live up to the covenants we make when we are baptized.

We were a rather wild bunch, but we stuck together. I have fond memories of life in Holbrook in the eighties. Both my parents worked at the radio station, so we were unleashed on the world at a young age.

My mother again says in her journal:

"The kids are all well...for now...since we just went through a rash of accidents. Bryan got hit in the mouth with a ball, Brady got poked in the eye and broke his collarbone, Bob fell off his bike and scratch his whole arm up, Holly broke her arm and got false appendicitis, and Maxer missed it all. Leah had pink eye and Dad hurt his foot on the motorcycle and the garbage cans blew up! Holly asked if Jesus was mad at us and if she was getting these things done to her because she had been bad! Bob came in complaining about a sore thumb and Holly said, 'Don't complain Bob. these are really blessings.' I don't know how they understand so much sometimes but they do."

Mom wrote about me getting poked in the eye and breaking my collarbone. Those are both good stories to describe my life in Holbrook at the time. The first one was getting poked in the eye. She didn't say that it was from a fight in school. Basically, I got an eye scratch and the other kid got more than that. Most fights in school tend to get broken up rather quickly, but not in Holbrook.

Fighting was a way of life back then. Growing up with three brothers we would fight a lot. That is when my dad taught us all to box. He showed us all the skills and we would practice on each other. My dad never openly told us to fight, but he did say, "If you get in a fight, you better win." We were taught not to be a victim, and to stick up for ourselves—and for each other.

We played baseball, rode bikes, skateboards, and motorcycles. I remember the first time I was in the paper. My brothers and I lashed tarps to our wrists and ankles and were jumping off a small cliff/hill in the high winds. We were loving it, and the local newspaper reporter just happened to be driving by at the time.

My father did not like to fish, and he hated to camp. But every year he and I looked forward to the church Father and Sons outing. It was always at Silver Creek in the White Mountains. These were Special times. We always came home with a bunch of trout for the family.

I have always loved the outdoors. I love fishing. It calms me down, and I was always bugging my dad to go. My mom and dad would take me to the lake and leave me there for an afternoon of fishing. I would always come back home with a full stringer of bluegill or catfish. Again this was the eighties and that is how people did things back then, especially with both parents working full time. We escaped to the big outdoor playground.

We didn't have much in the way of material things, but we had great examples in our parents. They both were hard working and involved in the community.

Dad supplemented the family income by being a DJ for dances in the area. Holbrook is not a very big town, so a lot of his dances were on the Navajo reservation and surrounding areas. So this along wit his travels as a sports broadcaster took him all around northern Arizona.

In addition to raising my brothers, sisters and me, my mother also worked at the radio station. She stretched the small amount of money that we did have a long way. She was—and still is—an amazing woman.

My siblings and I never knew how poor we were until later, but we made due and never felt any lack. Macaroni, government cheeses, and tomato juice soup were staples in the Busby house. And these meals always tasted so good, probably because they were served with love.

CHAPTER 3

Never a Dull Moment

In a small town there are few things to do, so I was active in baseball and school sports. Bryan was more of a jock, and I was the little brother who followed in his shadow. I didn't take sports very seriously, but I played. And when I wasn't playing sports, girls started to come into the equation.

Life was never dull and it often came with consequences.

I would fight a lot and so I visited the principal office frequently. This was at a time when the principals would still swat you, and I can recall the whistle of my principal's paddle to this day.

My siblings and I also had a game where we would close all the doors and cut out all the light in a small section of our three-bedroom, one-bathroom home. We would ball up socks in the end of another sock whack away at each other in the dark. It usually ended in blood.

Things started to get more serious as I grew older.

When I was thirteen I was involved in a pretty serious motorcycle accident. I had my first dirt bike when I was eleven. It was an old Honda four stroke trail bike that I wrecked into the fence in the backyard the first time I rode it. Eventually I was able to go and ride all over the hills and desert around Holbrook.

It was one day when my older brother Bryan and I were out riding that I got in a bad accident. I remember going about 40 or 50 mph trying to keep up with Bryan as we traveled down an old trail. We hit a spot where there were three jumps, and I was going too fast.

The first jump was fine. The second jump was a little less controlled. On the last jump, my front tire hit the berm and sent me flying through the air into an old barbwire fence. I do not remember much about the crash because I was knocked out. I had a helmet on that hit the fence post and then I was wrapped up in some barbwire. This was the first of many head injuries in my future.

My brother, Bryan, recalls another incident with a similar outcome:

> "We were going down the hill by Ann Marie's (his girlfriend) house, and you were trying to keep up with me and by the time I figured out you weren't with me, you had crashed pretty bad. I got back to you and couldn't put my bike down to help you up because I didn't have a kick stand. Somehow we got your bike started and we drove to the radio station so they could take you to the hospital. We found out you broke your collar bone."

We had some good times, too—times that weren't disrupted with injuries and blood. Those usually involved fishing at the lakes that are near the power plant to fish. I caught lots of catfish, bluegill, and carp that filled our freezer—and that no one would eat.

Rabbits and chickens usually came to the table instead.

We had lots of rabbit that my Grandpa Busby would raise for food. He also had a chicken coop, and when it came time to harvest the birds it was a family affair. Everyone had a job. Grandpa handled the ax. Bryan and I would chase down the chickens after that and get them into an old fifty-gallon drum. Bob's job was picking up the heads and disposing of them. Mom and Grandma were the chicken pluckers.

CHAPTER 4

Readjusting to Life on the Move

Eventually, we outgrew our house, and my dad got a better job in Mesa, Arizona. We were close to family again there, about a block or so from my aunt and uncle's house. Our home was a little bigger. We lived in a tight-knit mostly LDS community near Mesa High School and right around the block from our church.

Bryan attended high school, and I had to go back to middle school because Mesa High was only for 10-12th grade because the student population was so big. In Holbrook. I would have been a freshman at the high school there. I attended ninth grade at Taylor Junior High School. I rode the bus to and from school. We still didn't have a lot of money and my clothes were not as trendy as others.

I experienced my first real bullying episodes that year. It was a difficult time.

It got to the point that I had to talk to my dad about a specific kid that was doing most of the bullying. I was taught not to fight unless it was absolutely necessary, and if it was we'd better win.

My dad listened to me and gave me some advice that stuck with me all of my life. "Sometimes you have to do what you got to do." At fourteen years old that was a green light to stand up for myself. The following day went about the same, but when I stood up for myself for the verbal threats and told the kid where to go he then said, "You want to fight!"

The kid never knew what hit him as I unleashed the fury on him that day. I rode the bus home, covered in his blood, and suspended for two weeks. I also had a new-found respect from my peers. Needless to say, I wasn't bullied ever again. I did get in more fights through life, but I never lost—or I was still swinging when the fight was broken up.

I had a variety of friends from all over the place and different walks of life. My family was very inclusive with our friends. Our house was where everyone loved to hang out and eat. My parents' grocery bills were massive, I remember. We had "adopted" several friends over the years when we lived in that house and went to Mesa High. One we call Rookie (real name Jason) we took in and he has been a part of the family ever since.

While at Mesa High I did the high jump in track and played a lot of basketball and softball in city and church leagues. And of course, there were also my studies of the opposite sex!

I had picked up a few bad habits and had a bad boy/black sheep kind of thing going back then. I would drink in private and hide it from everyone. My view of myself and my attitude towards girls were very selfish. It was all about me and I didn't want to be held down by any rules.

Growing up in an LDS community, it was hard for me at this point in my life. This was before I knew what hard was. I made a lot of bad decisions back then, running away from home, sleeping in friends' parents RVs, and eating when I could. I had a bad relationship with my parents then and went through some rough years.

Then I got a wake-up call. I was working for a neighbor of my parents transporting cars from dealerships around the Phoenix and surrounding area. My friends and I drove a lot of cars to auto auction. One cloudy day when I was eighteen years old, I had picked up a new Chevy pickup that was stick shift and sporty.

While at a large intersection, we were all stopped at a red light. I was in the far-left lane and decided I to show off. I went through first, second, third, and fourth while spinning my tires and working my way into the intersection. Looking down at one point, I noticed the speedometer reading 55 mph on the dial and my back wheels began to drift. Panicking, I stomped on the clutch, the tires caught and shot me into oncoming traffic where I slammed into a semi-truck coming the other way.

I do not remember much after that, but the steering wheel and column slammed in with my chest, the dash smashed my knees and hand, and the windshield hit my forehead, and I took the rear view mirror off with my chin. My head was hurting and blood gushed all over the place. I was in shock so all I could think to do was hold my chin and slow the bleeding down. I do not remember the ride to the hospital or getting pulled out of the car, but I do know that other than some stitches in my chin I walked away from totaling that truck without a scratch. That is what I thought at the time, but in reality I had just suffered another serious concussion.

This gave me a chance to reassess my life. I knew I had to give up the girls and nightlife and focus on my family and my faith.

About six months later I was again in a serious car accident. This time it wasn't my fault but the driver's who rear-ended me. He was speeding and messing with his radio and never hit the brakes. I was stopped when I saw him coming and braced myself for the impact that left me with severe whiplash and an injured right shoulder. The hits kept coming.

CHAPTER 5

Reclaiming My Faith

My life revolved around physical therapy and appointments for a while after that. I was starting to become spiritual again and wanted to serve my church. I served an LDS mission in Oregon after the summer working. I remember doing my neck exercises the day I was opening my mission call. I was pretty pumped and did about five times the weight I was normally doing with my neck.

One thing that happened while I was in training at the missionary training center in Utah was I had a dream and woke up and wrote the dream down. The next day I figured out it was a system of encryption that I could use simple substitution of letters and characters to make a message unreadable unless you have the key. Little did I know at the time, but a career in cryptology was in my future.

It was hard work trying to spread the gospel of Jesus Christ. I taught about faith, repentance, and baptism by immersion. The few people that I did meet and teach will always have a place in my heart. We taught about Christ and his teachings. We believe in a plan where if we follow the commandments we can live with our family forever made possible by the atonement of Jesus Christ and covenants made between you and your Father in heaven.

Then I started losing weight. I have always been slim, but I was down a lot of weight. People would come up to me at church and tell me how sick I looked. After a trip to the doctor I found out that I had mononucleosis and had had it for months. I was so tired and could not get better, so I returned home after six months in the mission.

I left home weighing in around 180 pounds, but when I returned I was 137 pounds. I thought my mom was going to keep me tucked away in bed for months, but I slowly regained my strength and started back into normal life.

I had a close friend pass away in a car accident shortly after that. I did not take it well and kind of fell backwards for a while. I understand now that she would have wanted me to react the complete opposite and stay close to my faith.

Eventually, I landed a job working at a local television station. My dad got my foot in the door and before long I was working in the engineering department as a camera operator. I worked in that job for a couple of years before meeting my wife, Sarah.

The first time Sarah and I met I was showing off at the local community college playing volleyball, and we talked for the first time. She noticed a small tattoo on my left shoulder that I got when I was eighteen (another thing I didn't think through). She told her friends that she feels sorry for anyone who had to wake up and look at that every day. We started dating shortly after that and that was pretty much it.

Sarah has been through a lot over the last twenty-one years of marriage. We figured out that I was deployed or training for over seven years during our last twenty-one. She had to be strong and independent through all my Army career. She basically raised Ashley and Emma most of their early life. She also attended school and graduated from UCCS. She is now a high school social studies teacher.

CHAPTER 6

And the Two Shall Become One

Sarah and I were married on May 24, 1997. At that time, I worked in several capacities while I was at the television station to include audio and technical directing. I was very young to be doing that at just twenty-three years old.

Working at the television station had its perks. I was able to meet celebrities and politicians. I was actually working the audio booth when we were doing a satellite interview with now President Donald Trump. I had a small conversation with him while checking his microphone levels. I asked him for a million dollars, and he laughed He said he would be broke if he gave money to everyone who asked him for it.

My little family was starting to grow as well. My wife and I were expecting our first child and after much anticipation my sweet Ashley was born on February 4, 1999.

Sarah was in labor but kept getting sent home from the hospital for not being ready. It was a family event for the Busby clan. Everyone was excited because Ashley was the first granddaughter in our family. Jordan was the oldest grandson. He is my older brother Bryan's son. Sadly, he passed away when he was in a car accident at the age of three and a half. It was a big blow to the family and still is. I learned from my brother Bryan's strength. Little did I know that I would one day have to rely on modeling his behavior.

After finally getting the call from Sarah's doctor we moved the party to the hospital. The only time I have ever almost passed out was when I was holding Sarah still while they did the epidural. The nurse had me sit down because I was turning green. I am a little fuzzy about events, but when I tell friends who ask me what it was like I say, "It is the coolest and gross and nasty at the same time." A few of the things that I did as a new dad to be was make the mistake of eating corn nuts in the room with Sarah. I still hear about that from time to time. Yet our baby was born, and my sisters were all smiles and couldn't wait to see Ashley.

While at work in the engineering department at the television station, I had noticed a trend in the news of an impending fight and one night I was watching a live feed from Baghdad, when the United States was striking Iraq with tomahawk cruise missiles over something Saddam Hussein was doing. President Bill Clinton was in office at the time. I was interested in politics and did the news every day. I am very patriotic and would get fired up over things that other people wouldn't.

There was one CNN reporter who covers the Middle East there and she was on camera talking. She was not on the air, but I noticed that she was bad-mouthing the United States. She made me so upset. My colleagues in the engineering department didn't understand why I was so fired up.

I had thought about joining the military for a long time and never really acted on it. I was never a fan of following rules. Yet, I started really thinking about it and talked to a couple of recruiters about enlisting. It came down to the Army or the Air Force, but I didn't like how cocky the Air Force guy was.

I told the Army recruiter that I was driven by a strong desire to serve my country. A short time later, I enlisted as an E-1 PVT in the U.S. Army. I originally wanted to go into military intelligence, but the recruiter convinced me to avoid waiting for my top-secret clearance. Instead, he told me about a job where I would get a bonus if I joined a job where I could blow stuff up. My specialty was to be an Avenger crew member. My military occupational specialty 14S is in the Air Defense Artillery.

Much to my surprise, my wife supported me with the decision! I officially joined the Army a couple of weeks later. I knew in my heart that war was coming, and I didn't want someone to fight in my place, so I did what I felt was right at the time and enlisted. I gained a lot of experience that helped me to be a better officer later in my carrier.

CHAPTER 7

Army Life Begins

In March of 1999 I arrived at Fort Sill, Oklahoma, for basic training. I had travelled before, but only to a few states. California, Utah, New Mexico, and Oregon to name a few. I didn't know that my decision would take me around the world.

Basic training was physically and mentally challenging, but I had found my calling. I was good at being a soldier and took pride in it. I am still friends with guys who sucked it up there with me. It was towards the end of my basic training when the fighting broke out in Kosovo. I can remember thinking "here we go."

After my time at Fort Sill, I went on to learn my job in Fort Bliss, Texas. It turns out that I was good at being in the Army. I graduated top of my class and was awarded a live stinger missile to fire after my graduation ceremony. So, on a hot summer day on a portion of White Sands Missile Range I was able to track, engage, and destroy another dummy missile that was launched just before I engaged it.

It was nice to be there with Sarah, her mom, Charlotte, and baby Ashley. who did not like the sounds of the stingers taking off and exploding on target. She cried a lot, but was still the cutest baby.

After I graduated I was given thirty days of hometown recruiting, so I moved my things to Thatcher, Arizona, to be with Sarah and Ashley. They were living with her parents, Jack and Charlotte. Ashley was a loved little girl from the time she arrived. And I went fly fishing with Jack often to relax and to take in the beautiful surroundings.

I was originally taught to fly fish on a scout camping trip at Big Lake, Arizona. I had an old WWII Veteran as my scoutmaster. He made a big impression on me. I can still remember the first fish that I caught on a large dry fly that floats on top of the water. I remember the thrill I had when the fifteen-inch rainbow trout inhaled my fly. There was an epic fight that followed. I had to turn around and run up the bank to get it on shore. After that moment, I was hooked on the sport.

Other than an occasional lazy fishing trip for catfish or something like that I was fly fishing all the time. I found the water to be relaxing and calming just being outside enjoying nature.

Sarah's father Jack and I have a special relationship that came from the time we spent on the water. The hiking and hunting was good as well in the south east part of

Arizona. Jack and I both were in the doghouse on many occasions due to our love of these sports.

One of the times when Sarah and I fished on my honeymoon. The fishing was great on the trip, but my lovely new wife didn't like me spending all my time down in the water, while she stayed near the cabin after she got a ticket for not having a license.

The family cabin is in Oak Creek Canyon near Sedona, Arizona. The water is crystal clear and filled with catchable stocked rainbows and some nice brown trout. Trout do not live in ugly places. That's one reason I like to fish so much.

After returning to Fort Bliss, Texas, to wait for my secret security clearance, I found out that Sarah and I were going to have our second child. And even being pregnant again, she was excited when I received my orders for Fort Drum, New York. We then looked at a map and there on the lake just south of Canada was Watertown, New York. It would be home for the next several years.

The three of us stayed in a hotel for our first Christmas. The weather was so bad that I am sure that

Sarah was questioning living there. Yet, we ended up making some lifelong friends while we were stationed there.

When it came time for Emma to be born we went to the hospital and Emma came into our life on May, 25, 2000. She was a beautiful baby and her big sister Ashley was so proud.

Ashley and Emma were best friends growing up, and that made all the moves in the military that much easier, because they could always count on each other.

One good thing about upstate New York is the fishing. Whenever I was not training or at work I would try and get out to enjoy the outdoors and fly fish on many small streams in the Adirondacks and the Salmon River.

I spent a lot of time training at Fort Drum as we were getting ready to deploy to Kosovo. On top of lots of field time with my gunner, we would be instructed in Brazilian jujitsu. I excelled in the classes and once we starting doing crowd control techniques, I was chosen to be a snatch team leader.

That was the task of going out into the agitated crowd, subdue the individual causing the disruption, and drag them back behind the perimeter. Then we would flex cuff them and remove them to a secure area. I felt like we would be ready for anything.

As we were in our final training exercise, something happened that I will never forget. We were working with a team from the 82nd Airborne doing a training mission in the morning and I was sleeping before my next patrol when a solder came and told me that they could have used my Avenger a few minutes ago.

I asked him what he was talking about and that my patrol wasn't for a few hours. He then told me that a passenger jet hit one of the twin towers. I pulled out my television for recording footage from the FLIR to see if I could find a station that was broadcasting. After a few minutes, we were joined by a small group of soldiers watching the tower burning. Then the second jet hit the other tower. We all new at that moment that we were going to war.

Military life was hard on my family. My sweet Ashley and Emma were so small at that time, and my wife and I were trying to better our marriage, but it was difficult. Being home with Ashley and Emma by herself was hard on Sarah.

Besides the training I was traveling to the doctors at Walter Reed for TMJ, lock jaw, and chronic migraines. Sometimes I would be there for days, so I was soon proficient in the mass transit system. I was always taught that mission comes first, so I postponed a TMJ surgery and was given braces to stop my mouth from opening wide. All of this I did so I could go to Kosovo with my brothers in arms.

The month after September 11, 2001, I was heading to Kosovo with the 10th Mountain Division. We were on a "peacekeeping mission" for NATO. While we were in Kosovo the rest of the division went into Afghanistan. The attack on my country really lit a fire in me, and I wanted to fight.

Kosovo was a tough tour for me. The thing about Kosovo at that time was there was no air threat, so my Avenger system with its .50 caliber and stinger missiles were not really needed. I started pulling patrols, meeting with locals, and setting up and manning observation posts. I was basically acting as an infantry team leader.

My team and I lived in churches, patrolled a lot, and set up checkpoints. We would go back to Camp Bondsteel occasionally to restock on essential items, then would head back to whatever village, outpost, or small base we were living in at the time.

We first lived in an Albanian village near the town in Kosovo called Vitina, guarding a Serbian church and graveyard. It was not that bad of an assignment. We had tents with wood walls to live in, but we worked out of the church's morgue. I would actually enjoy telling my gunner ghost stories while he pulled security at night in the graveyard.

We had an area in the morgue that we turned into a place to eat, work out, and watch movies. We had a rat that we named Bobby. He would get up on the table and eat anything he could get his hands on. Bobby the Rat didn't care who was around.

I remember one night we were out on patrol and we stopped a car for being out past curfew. The very large Serbian passenger was being belligerent and obviously was drunk. When he placed his hands on my friends, you might say that I cracked a little smile before my jujitsu training kicked in. I took him down and subdued him by twisting his arm behind his back and with my knee on his neck.

On another particular snowy night while on a dismounted patrol in the town we were staying in, I noticed a figure in the field. It turned out to be the drunkest person I have ever met. He had thrown up and made a half a snow angel before giving up. From what we could understand in Serbian, he just wanted to go home.

We took him to the nearest home at about 1:00 in the morning, and the owner of the home showed us where the man lived. Needless to say, his wife and daughter were very upset at him when we dropped him off. The good-natured man that helped us then took us back to his home and made Turkish coffee for everyone.

We had many instances where I would interact with the locals and we didn't have any problems. Unless I had the wrong interpreter in the wrong town. It was sad to see the hate that was prevalent in the area.

One time, we checked out the area of a firefight and had to track the blood trails to the nearest town. No one there seemed to know what happened and actually covered up the blood trails with snow. The guy ended up being at the hospital when we found him.

I had another wake-up call while out patrolling the border with Macedonia. We were looking for smugglers bringing weapons and drugs back and forth between the border. While walking point of the patrol, I noticed a man approaching with a donkey with a pack on its back. We were all wearing our over white uniforms, so he didn't see us until I whistled to our new lieutenant.

Once he saw me raise my M-4 and point it at him, he slowly slid his hand up under the saddle of the pack mule. Right before I was going to pull the trigger, he responded to our shouts of "Stop or I will shoot" and raised his hands. Once we checked the mule, we found an empty pack and no weapons. He had probably just dropped off a load of something and was on his way back to town.

We followed his trail in the snow, and it led to an abandoned house. I went in to clear the home. It was clear, but trashed. There was a door leaning against the wall leading to the attic so I pulled myself into the attic. I noticed wiring running all over the place and when moving some clothes, I came face to face with a PMA-3 anti-personnel mine.

I didn't know if I was on a pressure plate with all the wires, so I got everyone out of the building and then slowly came down myself. The new lieutenant wanted a picture of it for EOD (explosive ordinance destruction) to come take care of it. I went back in and got the photo.

The same young officer almost sent me into a minefield to set up an observation post for the night. I asked about the recon of the area, and he said that everything was fine. I plotted the area on a minefield map and he had us right in the middle of one. While I was yelling at the lieutenant, our platoon sergeant came up to yell at me for yelling at him, I was a new sergeant at the time, but after he found out why he started to yell about it too. Tensions were high, to say the least.

After several months of this I started to rethink my military options. I found a reenlistment program where I could get a large bonus for switching to military intelligence. It was an easy choice for me, so I signed all the paperwork to make the change.

Then it was time to go home. I'll never forget the sight of Ashley running down the airport to give me a big hug when she saw me. Emma cried and didn't want anything to do with me because she didn't know who I was. She quickly figured it out and talked my ear off the whole way home. My girls were all so cute.

After returning to Fort Drum and a short stay at PLDC (leadership school for new E-5/sergeants). I received orders for intelligence training and moved my little family to Sierra Vista, Arizona. There they lived with Sarah's parents while I was away in school. Then it was time for me to head off for Korea.

Korea was interesting, as I had to do a year tour by myself. I started to paint in the barracks while everyone else was out and about. I painted a lot of landscapes that year. I was also promoted again, so when I returned from Korea I went straight to the basic noncommissioned officer course.

When I came down on orders for Fort Gordon, Georgia, I was excited to be a family unit again. I had basically been away from my family for two and a half years at that point. While there I was treated for six months of INH therapy because I was exposed to TB while in Kosovo and tested positive.

I didn't particularly like working in Georgia. I didn't like the weather, the fire ants, or my unit very much at the time. So when I had the chance to deploy to Iraq for the NSA I jumped on it.

I was part of the first Cryptologic Support Teams deployed to Iraq support the CJSOTF-AP. (Combined Joint Special Operations Task Force-Arabian Peninsula.) While there I worked with 5th and 10th Special Forces Group.

I was very productive at what I did and worked with various other agencies including the CIA and FBI. With the information I had, we were able to track down and kill or capture several High Value Targets. 10th Special Forces Group liked working with me so much that they requested me by name to come work in the Military Intelligence Detachment there.

My next military adventure was airborne school which I attended before moving my family to Colorado Springs, Colorado. I had always wanted to be an airborne paratrooper. I wished I was a little younger, and in better shape when I was going through school though because it hurt.

On my fourth jump with all my gear, I had a bad exit out of the aircraft over the drop zone. I didn't tuck my head, so the blast of air blew my helmet back and my risers got tangled up around my chest.

I started bicycling my legs like I was taught to spin out of it, but I was falling fast. My parachute finally opened and I had time to drop my equipment and hit the ground.

I hit my head very hard and had a pretty bad concussion, but I needed one more jump to graduate. I didn't want to start to over, so I sucked it up and jumped again the next day. I was sure to tuck my head on that jump.

Once I got to 10th Group, we were getting ready to deploy to Iraq again. After a couple more months with the family I deployed on my second tour in Iraq, as part of a regular rotation with 5th Group.

There was a considerable amount of mortars and rockets that would hit our base. The first time I heard them come in and I remember thinking, "Someone is actually trying to kill me right now." It was a surreal feeling.

During my time home in Colorado Springs. I would go fly fishing and get back to the water. It helped me to relax and decompress after my deployments. I also spent time with my girls.

My third tour in Iraq was a little different. I was selected to become a sergeant first class/E-7 and was also working on my Warrant Officer packet. My commander at the time, Col. Ken Tovo (now General Tovo), wrote my letter of recommendation. I submitted that with all of my evaluation reports and brief description about myself to the Warrant Officer selection board.

I was very productive at my job and worked with another SGT dismantling networks of terrorist and Shia militias. We had a nickname of the killer Bees, because both of our last names started with B.

I also injured my back on my last tour in Iraq. All the wear and tear on my body had started to take a toll. I was also lifting weights every day for about two hours a day. I bulged a disk out in my back while working out in the gym one day. It was sore for a week or so, but I recovered quickly. I didn't know it at the time, but my lower back was going to play a crucial role in my future.

CHAPTER 8

The Travails of War

After returning to Fort Carson, I was diagnosed with PTSD from the things I had seen and done. They medicated me for sleep and anxiety and left me to the 10th Group doctors to follow up.

The 10th Special Forces Group doctors didn't get that logic, so they just kept me medicated until I eventually left the unit.

I was selected to go to Warrant Officer Candidate School and left for that shortly after returning to Colorado. After I graduated from school, I returned back to Colorado Springs, CO to be with my family again. There was only one position in the entire 10th Special Forces Group that did my new job, and the Chief Warrant Officer in the position was not leaving. My new branch manager wanted to give me a break from deployments, so I received orders for Wiesbaden, Germany.

Sarah, Ashley, and Emma fell in love with Germany—right after getting over the jet lag. Ashley and Emma were able to travel all around Europe. We have so many memories from our time in Germany. We spent time in the Canary Islands one year, and actually got to stay a few extra days due to the big volcanic eruption in Iceland. Ashley and I went to London one year to see the Phantom of the Opera in the original theater. We had a great time seeing the British museum as well as all the other tourist's attractions.

Two months after I arrived at the unit I herniated my disk in my back. Even heavily medicated, I deployed to Afghanistan a couple months later. My time in Afghanistan started out in Baghram Air Base. I was assigned as a liaison between my military intelligence unit and the theater command group. I had a daily briefing to do and sitting at a desk most of the time, so the ninety Percocet a month I was taking didn't have much of an effect on my performance.

After returning from my first deployment to Afghanistan, I was constantly in doctor appointments. I began getting my nerves cauterized so I couldn't feel the injury, steroid injections, and tons of opiates to get me deployable again.

Sarah and the girls were all at the middle school at that time. Sarah had her degree in political science so she would work as a substitute and eventually got a position as a paraprofessional working with special needs children.

My kids, however, weren't fairing so well.
Deployments had taken a toll on them, and then there was
life in the modern world. Ashley was bullied in middle
school. I think she was a target for bullies because she was
so nice, and it was starting to get to her. If I knew how
much she was bothered by it, I would have pulled rank on

the parents of the children. It wasn't the eighties anymore, so she couldn't handle things like I did back in the day.

Bullying is so bad and I think girls are worse than boys. They can be mean and much more into mental bullying.

When Ashley first started school, we gave her a big pair of cubic zirconia earrings. We were living in Augusta, Georgia, at the time. Later that day another girl came up to her and almost ripped it out of her ear. She had a gash in her ear, but nothing was ever done.

I had no idea how all of this would affect her later in her life. She was usually such a positive person.

I then returned to the U.S. to do some special training. I was to be the Officer in Charge of a small, highly specialized team that focused on targeting. It was nice to grow my beard out and run around doing our thing. At one point, I acquired the nickname of Rasputin. I had a very good team, and we set a high bar of success on my second tour in Afghanistan.

I was very serious about my mission there. I was still working out and staying in shape when my cauterized nerves started growing back together. I was on OxyContin at this point. I used it two times a day, rather than all the Percocet I had been taking. I had also herniated a disk in my neck that also kept me in constant pain.

Despite all of the medication I was on, my team was very successful during that time. We still had the occasional mortars and rockets coming in. We had some suicide bomber blow himself and the gas truck he was driving up at the gate to my forward operating Base (FOB).

I just heard it, saw the smoke and what was left, but I was dealing with the situation fine. I lived my life living in my office, using water bottles for showering, and going to the bathroom in a porta-potty. Every once in a while a friend would take me to the other side of the base to get showered and eat in the chow hall. I had some great friends who would take me to the gym and shower on their Gators (side by side ATVs).

It was very hot in Afghanistan in the summer. I remember them checking a thermometer in the shade one day and it was 130 degrees. My office consisted of two metal shipping containers, and I burned myself several times just by touching the metal on accident.

We did most of our missions at night, so it really was bad when you woke up in the middle of the day to use the bathroom or to find out the AC unit went out.

We had a rodent problem in Afghanistan as well. I made a better mouse trap out of a trash can, water bottle and some string. It worked well.

I was a big punisher fan, and that skull symbol was everywhere. I also got a new nickname because I was so intense when I was doing my job. It was "Vlad the Impaler" and I didn't mind.

After returning to Germany after that tour I was right back in to see pain management. They put me on methadone this time and recauterized my nerves in six places in my back and six places in my neck. Once I was in good enough condition to deploy, I went back for my third trip to Afghanistan.

Before I had to leave, I was in Texas training and I was able to visit with some of my family. I saw my brother Bob who just happened to be taking care of my dog Gooch while I was in Germany. I also was there to see my cousin have her baby, so I was able to spend time with that side of my family.

My aunt had taken me in after I moved to California when I was eighteen or nineteen years old. I was very close with them all. When it came time for me to leave, we decided to go out for dinner. After dinner we were saying our goodbyes, and I started to let the "what if" thoughts start to get to me. *What if I don't make it back this time?* I could tell my PTSD was bothering me, but it was mission first.

CHAPTER 9

An Abrupt End

My third tour was a hard one and the one that brought my career to an end. After over a year in the WTU, I was retired at the age of thirty-eight. I couldn't work or do much of anything and the stress of not having me home had strained my relationship with Sarah. Therapy had not worked up to that point. It was a very hard transition from the military back to civilian life. We were basically homeless for the summer while visiting family. At one point I had to take out a personal loan to keep us on our feet waiting while all my different pays were set up.

I am 100% disabled, so getting my new normal was difficult for me, and also my family. Ashley and Emma had travelled all over the world as military brats, so they were starting at new schools and trying to make new friends. They had been there for each other their whole lives though.

I took my pain management into my own hands once moving back to Colorado and finally got off the opiates. In June of 2012, I went to see a doctor to try medical marijuana (MMJ). After about six months of using it, I was forced to choose between MMJ and the opiates they still had me on. For me it was an easy decision.

My doctor in Germany gave me five years to live in November 2011 due to all the medication I was taking, so switching to a plant that replaced all of my pain killers, muscle relaxers, and other medications was the best decision for me. The decision was made before I even moved from Germany as I had talked about the cannabinoid system with my doctors and religious leaders prior to moving back to Colorado. I have been on medical marijuana everyday sense. I am back to walking normal without the use of my cane anymore. I am down to the minimal amount of PTSD medication I have to be on to keep me level. My quality of life has improved, and I am finally off the opiates that the government kept shoveling down my throat to keep me deployable.

I decided that to help pay the rent and get some more income I would go back to school using the GI Bill. I attended UCCS to get a degree in geography and environmental studies and a minor in geology.

Having a brain injury and going to school is one of the hardest things I had done up to this point in my life. I can't read very well and have serious short-term memory problems. I was in a very bad place in this part of my life.

At that point, Sarah had told me she was leaving me and taking the kids. I had gone from being a subject matter expert military intelligence officer to feeling stupid and like I was a nobody. It seemed like I had no other choice than to take my own life like so many of my brothers and sisters in arms have done before. I was home alone, and I had enough medicine to kill an elephant. I was at my weakest point I have ever been in my life and I only saw one way out.

Just then my wife's little old Shih-Tzu Belle came walking up to me and started licking me. I had been crying and at that moment I felt like someone loved me. I focused on the dog and started to come to the realization that everything was going to be alright. I was not alone.

I believe in guardian angels and know that someone was there with me when I needed strength. I believe I was protected and watched over through my life. There are specific moments in my life that I can't explain, and this was one of them.

I finally got my pay figured out and that helped a lot with the stress. Sarah had been student teaching, and she got a full-time teaching position at the high school. She was less stressed as well. I was tutored for my math class as I was not comprehending the equations and started to work with the disability office at UCCS where I was going to school. I also had a purpose every school day. I took Ashley and Emma to school.

I also had the occasional fly-fishing trip to keep me occupied. It was at this point that I was introduced to a non-profit organization called Project Healing Waters Fly Fishing (PHWFF). The chapter in Colorado Springs is the second largest in the country.

CHAPTER 10

Healing Waters

Project Healing Waters Fly Fishing is an organization started at Walter Reed hospital by a man named Ed Nicholson. He was there getting treatment for cancer when he would see all of these soldiers with physical and mental health issues sitting around or in their rooms.

He decided to get some of them out and teach them how to cast a fly rod. From there it went to fly tying, rod building, and lots of fly fishing. Now Project Healing Waters is in all fifty states and across the world.

When I went on my first trip with them I could feel the

respect, thanks, and love that we all received. The fishing was unbelievable and I had to pick up my fly fishing skills to fight and land some of the biggest fish of my life.

I have said it before, but I felt more like my old self whenever I was out on the water. I have met some amazing people including Ed Nicholson, the founder of Project Healing Waters Fly Fishing. He knew my story and one night we had a surprise firework show that really set my PTSD off. The next thing I remember is his hand on my shoulder and him telling me everything was going to be all right. He helped me ground myself and recognize the surroundings.

In time, I adjusted somewhat to life in college. Life at home improved, and I began retraining my brain to think a different way. I started fly fishing more, and I was getting better.

I became an active member of Project Healing Waters. It was a great coping mechanism for me. I found that when I was fishing I didn't have as much anxiety. I wasn't on high alert, and I started to feel more and more like my old self. Volunteering with other vets helped take my mind off of my own issues. I learned that I wasn't the only person who had seen and done things they wish they hadn't. Things you can't unsee.

I graduated from UCCS in December 2015 with my degree in Geography and Environmental Studies and a minor in Geology.

I was chosen to go on a national PHWFF trip in Tennessee and made lifelong friends and connections. I also was invited on a few other trips as well. I've learned a lot about the organization, like only 1% of the money raised goes to overhead and running the organization. Everything else is done by volunteers and hosts and by people's generosity.

The fly fishing community in Colorado Springs is very supportive of their active and veteran military members. Ed is an amazing person and fellow veteran. One of the main fundraising events for PHWFF in Colorado Springs is the Fly-Fishing Film Tour (F3T).

I was asked to speak and share some of my story during the event. I did it in front of a sold-out crowd of over 500 people. I could never have imagined doing something like that, but I made it through. I then did it

again a couple weeks later in Silverthorne, Colorado. We
raised around $60,000 during the two events for the
program that year.

CHAPTER 11

The End of Innocence

I continued to drive my girls to school all this time. Ashley was in high school and Emma was not far behind her. Ashley had been through a lot with everything in her life. She loved art and singing and nature. I remember her always having pets dogs, snails, hamsters, a rabbit that had crazy teeth and liked to escape, and things like snails. She wanted to study invertebrates in college. She graduated from high school in May 2017.

I then started driving her to college. She decided to attend a local community college instead of going away to school.

She was also dealing with PTSD from a sexual assault when she was sixteen. A supposed friend—we know who it is, he knows who I am talking about as well— snuck into

Ashley's room and raped her. He then spread vile rumors to his friends at the school. The boy was from our LDS Church ward here in Colorado Springs. There are several things about this kid that have come to light from other schools. It wasn't his first nor his last act of violence.

Before we knew the extent of the assault, we reached out to the parents of the boy. They declined to talk to us. So, I took Ashley to file a police report. It wasn't enough to set her on the path to healing.

She had many people at school and church who cared for her, but she never saw it. She did meet with our bishop at the time a lot, but stopped going to all of church because of the rumors and she didn't feel comfortable anymore. She would come to the first part of the meeting to take the Sacrament, but then she would go home. Sarah and I were fine with that.

She would frequently be in the counselors' office in high school to have some herbal tea and relax. The office staff and teachers were wonderful at the school. She did continue to be bugged by people who were probably just jealous, but also from all the rumors that had been spread around about her.

She was a very strong, beautiful and talented girl. She had a team of doctors and lots of friends who helped her out so much. She even found herself a sweet heart, and they were planning their life together.

She had attempted suicide before several times, but I was always able to stop her. On March 15, 2018 she got so down that she could not get out of it. Her own personal demons drove her to take her own life.

I take medication for nightmares and sleep at night and am normally deep asleep for about eight hours. That morning around 4 a.m. I woke up to the screams from Sarah to call 911. She had found Ashley. As I ran with my phone down the stairs she tried to stop me but continued screaming. While talking to the 911 operator I went into Ashley's room and I found her in her closet. I checked for a pulse, but when I touched her she was already cold. While I was crying, I was able to cover her body with a blanket while I continued to talk to the 911 operator. The police and first responders were there soon and escorted me out of the room.

As I sat on my couch with my whole world upside down, I tried to remember if I told her I loved her. In my foggy memory, I remembered that I had that night before she went to bed. I went down to check if she had a ride to school the next day and told her I loved her. She told me that she loved me and I went to bed not knowing what I would be doing less than six hours later.

As we sat talking to police and fireman and our local church leaders, things felt detached, like this could not be happening. "Not to me and my family." Our friends and church leaders who showed up to help us get through the first day were invaluable.

My parents were on the first flight out of Phoenix to get to us. They were the first to arrive. By the time all of my and Sarah's family had shown up we had over fifty direct family members at her memorial service.

Ashley's talents were on display during the memorial service in the form of her art work. She picked up painting from me after I couldn't do it anymore due to the shakiness of my hands. She was self-taught except for getting into AP Art her senior year.

We started a scholarship fund in her name to give to deserving students from her high school every year for the rest of our lives and hopefully longer. It will go to two deserving students from Liberty High School who excel in the arts and sciences. Ashley loved both.

Life is different now. I started writing this to get my story out and to share my sweet Ashley's story. Friends have told me that not only is this something that is therapeutic for me, but it could also help out other people who are dealing with their own personal issues. We all have them.

I pray that our story will touch someone and let them know that they are loved. I hope people going through hardships will find inspiration from this.

I still am very active in Project Healing Waters and have found that service for others has been one of the best things for me. I see the joy and excitement from everyone I teach to fly fish and that brings me a sense of calm and satisfaction. Again, trout don't live in ugly places.

Colorado has so many places to fish and enjoy the outdoors. One of our favorite places to go around the state is Rocky Mountain National Park. There is a particular place near Glacier Basin that we like to camp. It is close to fishing, hiking, and has plenty of chances to see wildlife. I also like to fish the South Platte river as well.

Whenever I am fly fishing I am always doing something. Tying on leaders, rigging rods, tying flies on the tippet and trying tactics to fool the fish to eat your particular pattern. There is little time to think of anything else. For me that works.

I have found something that helps me to keep my mind occupied, but knowing that through my savior Jesus Christ's atonement and resurrection I will see Ashley again. That brings me peace and comfort.

I received an email recently from a participant on a Project Healing Waters trip and things like this keep me going:

Brady,

Words cannot express my appreciation for your assistance and camaraderie on Saturday. I have had great days fishing before, but nothing compares to the Saturday experience. If I can ever return the favor assisting you in an endeavor you take on, please let me know. I look forward to meeting you again.

Brothers in Arms,
Ron

Everyone copes with death and traumatic experiences differently. I feel at peace on the water. I have decided to start to paint again in Ashley's honor. I find that when I am in quiet tender moments I can feel her near. I know that through Jesus Christ we all can be resurrected and united with our loved ones.

I am writing this memoir not only as a tribute to Ashley, but also with a hope that others can learn from this experience. That people can have hope that things can get better. I will never forget my daughter, Ashley, and I wish everyone hurting will find their Healing Waters.

A Tribute to Ashley

Ashley Lynne Busby

February 4, 1999 - March 15, 2018

Ashley returned to the safe loving arms of her Savior on March 15, 2018.

Our sweet Ashley Lynne Busby was born on February 4, 1999 in Mesa Arizona to Brady and Sarah Busby. Shortly after she was born, her dad joined the Army and they began their adventure as a military family. Her sister Emma was born just a year after Ashley. They were especially close and share a special bond being each other's rock wherever they landed. As part of a military family, she traveled to several countries and made close friends around the world who remain very dear to her.

Ashley was a talented artist. She carried a sketch book with her at all times and could produce an incredible piece in minutes. Ashley loved to sing, and performed with her high school chamber and jazz choirs. She could often be heard in her bedroom playing the ukulele and singing her favorite songs.

Ashley was always curious and wanted to know about everything, especially animals. She fell in love with the study of invertebrates in fourth grade when she kept pet snails. This love continued as she took biology and zoology classes in high school. In college, she was studying to become a malacologist, a scientist who studies mollusks. Ashley had a strong desire to make a difference in the world.

As we mourn the death of our sweet daughter, sister and friend, we are comforted to know that she is in the arms of her loving Savior, Jesus Christ. We are grateful for the knowledge of the atonement and resurrection.

She leaves behind her dad Brady, mom Sarah, sister Emma, and her sweetheart Trevan. Ashley also leaves behind numerous grandparents, aunts, uncles, cousins, dogs, snails, fish, and other various creatures.

Donations in Ashley's memory can be made to the Ashley
Busby Memorial Scholarship Fundashleybusby.org

Published in *The Gazette* on Mar. 21, 2018

ABOUT THE AUTHOR

Brady Busby is currently a part-time fly fishing guide for the Peak Fly Shop in Colorado Springs. He is a very active member of Project Healing Waters Fly Fishing, and enjoys the time spent on the water and the camaraderie of being surrounded with other veterans who have shared experiences and hobbies.

Brady is available to speak about his experiences both on and off the water.

For more information visit his website at: https://healingwatersbook.com

36238362R10083

Made in the USA
Middletown, DE
13 February 2019